whirlwind of words

Loren Allen

BookLeaf Publishing

Presentation by *BookLeaf Publishing*

Web: www.bookleafpub.com

E-mail: info@bookleafpub.com

ISBN: 978-93-95784-06-1

First edition 2022

DEDICATION

This book is dedicated to anyone that finds a piece of themselves within the pages - you are not alone. Stay strong.

ACKNOWLEDGEMENT

Thank you to my friends and family, for being an optimum support system throughout my time writing.

Thank you to my English teachers (Mr. Sisson and Ms. Choudhury) for always believing in me and taking the time to nurture and develop my creative ability.

Thank you to the author that inspired me throughout this journey (Sabrina Benaim).

PREFACE

As someone who has struggled with mental illness my whole life, I am an advocate of speaking up and asking for help.

Personally, I'm aware of how hard it can be to discuss how you're feeling and how your thoughts can hold you captive within your own mind.

Normalise the struggle that you go through. Let's reduce and defeat the stigma around mental health.

step by step: tea

my cup of tea

soaking in honey, suckling the leftover love that
drips from your honeycomb -
does that make me the queen bee?

watching as the transparent steamy water fills
with a rich colour reminds me of you,
how you filled my life with rich emotions; my
first love, comfort, tea
yet, standing by and watching as the tea bag
stills does not help the liquid stay warm

the shapeshifter

hope often showcases itself in numerous forms,
picture it as a shapeshifter; constantly switching
appearances in hope (ironic) that we don't give
up on ourselves
i have been presented with the everchanging
shape of hope on numerous occasions, yet still
never certain when they will next appear
they have been a single flower, sprouting
between the cracks of the pathway, almost
impossible, without soil, without water,
seemingly existing against all odds
they have been a song, speaking so truly to
every fiber of my being that it reminds me i am
not as alone as i perceive myself to be
they have been good news, ringing in my ears
like a wedding church bell, loud and deafening
but never ceasing to make me smile
they have been a message from a near-stranger
on a trashy dating app i downloaded on a whim
at 18, hoping to find a version of love i have yet
to experience
but,
most importantly,

hope has always been present in the depths of
my heart, in my head, waiting, yearning to be
noticed, to be needed, to fulfill its purpose
hope is everywhere you need it to be,
but they will never make us search too far,
hope accompanies you, always.
create your magic.
make your mark.
your story deserves to be heard.

midnight drive

in my field of work, people fly pass like cars in
traffic - they stay for a while but leave once they
get given the chance to, once the light grants
them the pleasure of fleeing; a lot of aspects in
my life are like stand-still traffic - a long
agonising wait before succeeding in moving
forward
wait
scrap that thought; my life only has the agony of
waiting, i'm missing the success
god, next week was really exhausting

three (3) hours

meditate for 15 minutes, twelve times

but that equals 3 hours

so maybe just six times

or three

or maybe more because i just drank
9 cups of coffee and my teeth
feel fuzzy and my tongue is
dancing more gracefully than my body
ever could

is this really living?
or just existing?

thank (i love) you

you make me not want to want to die.
I love you.

you're the first flower that blooms in the spring.
I love you.

i'd use all of my emotional scars from the past to
carve out a single smile from your lips.
your lips are like sour strawberry laces; they
make my jaw ache and laugh, but they are so
sweet that i wouldn't have it another way.
i'd save up my pocket money as a kid to buy
strawberry laces like you.

when i picture a church, i no longer see myself
in an open casket upon walking in.
I see you.
stood at the end of an aisle, quite similar to the
supermarket, waiting for me.
but, we're not shopping for avocados.

you make the lonely nights less lonely.
granted, they've never actually been lonely. i've always been taunted by the dark thoughts flying around in my head like the stack of papers i once dropped in the school corridor in 2014.
but,
this is safe.

you give me this feeling that i can conquer the world.
granted, i can't conquer the actual world, but you're my world.
and i hope i conquer you.
because you make me not want to want to die.
anymore.
you make this shitty existence worth something.

i love you is my way of saying thank you.

knowledge off a duck's back

it's a dog eat dog world and i'm not even a cat;
i'm a duck
waddling through life whilst people feed me
something i struggle to digest
that something being knowledge rather than
bread
sure I can consume the knowledge but cannot
digest it

yet, the saddest thing is that you have spent your
whole life believing that ducks need bread
just as we believe
we need knowledge

pressure

The stress is overwhelming - this is my break. My head hurts, my body aches and my eyes are closing without my conscious demand. I can't remember the last time I felt relaxed; last night I got 4 (four) hours of sleep - it was probably then.

I am DRAINED.

I have a list of to-dos taller than my motivation to do them. I really need these grades. Without them, I'm nothing. All I've ever known is grades - A is good, B is okay, anything else is not. Anything below a C is a failure.
I'm so used to being contantly assessed that I'm beginning to grade myself.
Getting out of bed - D.
Doing some work - B.
Crying - U.
No matter what I do, I can't get an A in life.

Maybe that's because I don't have one.

I feel like a machine - constant information being programmed and store as if I have the capacity to remember it all.
Maybe I'm faulty.
Maybe the factory gave me the wrong parts.
I'm not even an A grade robot, does that make me worthless?
Because that's what it feels like.

I'm stuck in a routine.
Wake up, work, sleep.
The only problem is, I'm missing that last step every time. I never feel asleep. Even when I am sleeping, my brain is active - I dream of failure a lot. My brain has labeled itself as a waste of time, a product that wasn't yet ready to be put on the market, but they did anyway.
That's state crime for you.

I wonder if my teachers ever see me as a person.
Maybe they are robots, too. Upgraded ones.
Maybe updates happen during your 20s. I'm in need of one. Even now my wrist is clicking - I must have a loose bolt or wire somewhere.

Send me back to the factory.

spring in bloom

i still remember you as a little girl -
overwatering the flowers because you never
knew how to stop giving.

but, did you leave enough water for yourself?

plant the seed of love within your heart,
and watch it grow.

then water it with a little too much sadness,
and watch it die.

the death of my sanity

the panic attacks came first, Anxiety wrapped it's hands around my throat until i could no longer breathe - giving me a few minutes of normality before doing it again
and again
until i became pliant and submissive under it's fingertips, willing and obeying, letting it ruin my life.

the dark thoughts came second, winning and showcasing it's silver medal whilst i'm curled up in the corner of my room, my home, where i'm supposed to feel safe and protected, willing the suicidal thoughts to leave me be, to let me be happy, to stop destroying the little ounce of serotonin i have left.

the dismorphia was the last to join the group, it pulled up a chair, hung up a mirror and started to distort the way i looked. not only that, it brought a friend. a friend of it not of me. one that hated when my stomach was full, one that sobbed when a pair of old jeans no longer fit, one that

still sticks around, slowly destroying the
self-love that i worked so hard for.

and as i slowly lost faith, in myself, in my
future, in humanity, the trio only grew stronger.

triggering the death of my sanity.

a letter to a(n) (ex)lover

you're Keeping me awake, as not even one of my most wildest dreams can make me smile as much as you do
You removed all the air from my lungs - i can't help but bark out a ridiculous unfiltered laugh when you tell one of those infamous jokes that other people don't seem to appreciate
i can't believe how much you've changed my Life, the impact you've had on me will never compare to another. the smile on my lips never faults when you are around.
your Eyes show every single emotion that runs through your body, leaving me speechless whenever our gazes meet. so warm, so kind, so loving. tenerife sea.

survived another year

birthdays: days in which one blows out some candles in order to be granted a wish on the annual anniversary of their first intake of breath. birthdays: days in which family and friends gather with the main aim of making you happy. birthdays: days all about an individual whose wishes seem to be granted by blowing onto candlelight which flickers within the darkness, basking light on their greatness.

who needs a wish when you exist?
who needs one single day to celebrate my sad excuse of an existence when you steal the breath in my lungs, paint a smile on my face, and make all of this worth enduring?

i miss seeing your face behind the camera, snapping an in-motion photograph of my saliva hitting the cake as i blow so strongly to kill each and every little flame, feeling triumph as you cheer me on.

i have lost count of how many i have celebrated
without you.

i have lost count of how many of my wishes
were wasted on wishing to have you back.

celebrations don't feel the same without you.

i have simply been surviving each day since
you've been gone.

thought dump

numb. never looks both ways before crossing the street. never actively tries to die, yet no longer care if he does. broken. heart split in two, shattered, scattered with the remains of a man he used to be. emotionless psychopath. emotions? never heard of them. aimlessly wandering, or wandering aimlessly? both. neither. who knows, anymore? no body. detached in a world where everyone basis their self-worth on how many people care for them. alone. walls surrounding my own thoughts, but i am not claustrophobic. maybe that's part of the problem. i used to dream of being so strong nothing could shake me, but this is no dream. this is a nightmare, a nightmare that sweeps me up in it's arms every night and reminds me that i am alone. numb. drowning. bodies are cars. we introduce ourselves as our bodies, but what really matters is the engine. the mind. i am losing mine fast; i have never been much of a runner.

late night thoughts

02:48
08/07
my anxiety is such a big part of who I am - it's been around forever and has affected how i've grown and the person i've become. if i fix it, then will i even be me? will he still love me? will i still love me? will i feel a stranger in someone's body? just an empty nothingness..?

professional actress

when you spend all day pretending to be
someone else you start to forget who you really
are

stitching cut out patches of personalities together

the only way i feel accepted is to mirror and
mimic others

are my interests really my own?

are any of my experiences original?

i'm tired of pretending.

i can't stop.

i don't know how.

i don't know who i am.

natural disaster

constant volcanic eruption of emotions;
earthquakes of anger
tornados of frustration
tsunamis of tears
a whole village of dreams and hopes washed
away
destroyed daily
building from scratch, pretending it never
happened
how tiring it can be to overcome a natural
disaster

shifting realities

the main problem is not that i want my favourite fictional characters to be real,
but that i want to be fictional.

i don't want to bring my comfort characters into the terrible world we live in.

i want to live in theirs.

i want a world full of magic. full of selfless heroes. full of epic love stories that will go down in history.

i want to be fictional.

a hopeless hopeful

and with that one single look
the pain
the frustration
the anger
it all melts away

hopelessly deeply truly in love with the one who
knows my deepest darkest thoughts, feelings,
desires, secrets

begging for them not to begin the destruction

begging for them not to press the self destruct
button i have kept hidden for so many years

they're in love with a hopeless romantic
i'm in love with a hopeful disaster

first born, first forgotten

the first born,
the eldest,
the one everyone relies on.

being the eldest sibling has to be one of the
toughest things,
you give up your childhood experiences and take
on all the trauma and sadness and make it yours.
our parents will never understand the sacrifices
we make just to keep everything glued together,
so no one could see the cracks in the foundation
-
no one, but us.

the eldest sibling always has the worst mental
health.
they have bad trust issues,
they shut everyone out because they learned
from a young age how to solve their problems
alone.

they are a people pleaser,
a hopeless romantic,
they get attached too easily,

a burst of shining sunshine on the outside, but a rainstorm within.

have a bunch of hobbies as a coping mechanism,
completely burnt out but still pushing
themselves to do better -
to make people proud

they did and do everything they can to create a safe atmosphere within these four walls

but even with four walls
it's still a broken home

the one everyone relies on,
the eldest,
the first forgotten.

the open wound

the deepest pain i ever felt
was denying my own feelings
to make everyone else comfortable

the deepest regret i ever felt
was not speaking out and asking for help
in fear that i would be a burden

pain changed me.
it made me trust less and overthink more.
it made me shut people out.
it taught me how to smile and pretend that i'm
okay
when deep down my heart is breaking
into a thousand pieces
as i desperately try to hold myself together.

i am so exhausted from pretending that i am
okay,
of taping up a forever open wound.

the next chapter

it can be hard
to turn the page
not knowing what to expect

but that's part of the adventure

you are the main character

each year you go on
is a brand new chapter

write your own story
be who you need to be
who you want to be

what will be in store for you next?

the only way to find out is to
keep going

www.ingramcontent.com/pod-product-compliance
Lightning Source LLC
Chambersburg PA
CBHW051753130826
49812CB00033B/1135
9789395784061